I0813179

DISCOVERING THE UNITED STATES

Utah

BY BLYTHE LAWRENCE

An Imprint of Abdo Publishing
abdobooks.com

abdobooks.com

Printed in China.
052024
092024

Cover Photo: Shutterstock Images
Interior Photos: Olivier Morin/AFP/Getty Images, 4–5; Shutterstock Images, 6 (top left), 6 (top right), 9, 10, 12–13, 14, 18, 24, 28 (middle left); Michael Sy/Shutterstock Images, 6 (bottom left); Mc Photo/Alamy, 6 (bottom right); Tomas Nevesely/Shutterstock Images, 11, 28 (bottom left); Alex Goodlett/Getty Images Sport/Getty Images, 17; Piola666/E+/Getty Images, 20; Sean Pavone/Shutterstock Images, 22–23; Bettmann/Getty Images, 26; Allison J. Hahn/Shutterstock Images, 28 (top left); Red Line Editorial, 28 (top right), 29; Peter Kunasz/Shutterstock Images, 28 (bottom right)

Editor: Marley Richmond
Series Design: Katharine Hale

Library of Congress Control Number: 2023949373

Publisher's Cataloging-in-Publication Data

Names: Lawrence, Blythe, author.
Title: Utah / by Blythe Lawrence
Description: Minneapolis, Minnesota: Abdo Publishing, 2025 | Series: Discovering the United States | Includes online resources and index.
Identifiers: ISBN 9781098294151 (lib. bdg.) | ISBN 9798384913429 (ebook)
Subjects: LCSH: U.S. states--Juvenile literature. | Utah--History--Juvenile literature. | Western States (U.S.)--Juvenile literature. | Physical geography--United States--Juvenile literature.
Classification: DDC 973--dc23

All population data taken from:
"Estimates of Population by Sex, Race, and Hispanic Origin: April 1, 2020 to July 1, 2022." *US Census Bureau, Population Division*, June 2023, census.gov.

CONTENTS

Fireworks exploded to celebrate the beginning of the 2002 Olympic Winter Games.

The Olympic State

More than 50,000 people gathered in a stadium in Salt Lake City, Utah. It was 2002. The Olympic Winter Games were about to begin. Lively music started to play. The crowd clapped and cheered as athletes paraded into the stadium.

Utah Facts

DATE OF STATEHOOD
January 4, 1896

CAPITAL
Salt Lake City

POPULATION
3,380,800

AREA
84,897 square miles
(219,882 sq km)

STATE BIRD

California seagull

STATE TREE

Quaking aspen

STATE FLOWER

Sego lily

STATE ANIMAL

Rocky Mountain elk

Each US state has a different population, size, and capital city. States also have state symbols.

Athletes waved flags from their home countries. Then came the grand finale. Athletes from the winning 1980 US men's ice hockey team lit the Olympic cauldron. Olympic rings glowed in the middle of the stadium. The crowd cheered.

Seventy-seven nations took part in the 2002 Olympic Winter Games. The Opening Ceremony kicked off this historic event. The ceremony celebrated Utah and the rest of the United States.

Utah's Land

Utah is located in the West region of the United States. Idaho and Wyoming are to the north. Nevada lies to the west. Colorado is to the east. Arizona is to the south. Utah's southeast corner touches the northwest corner of New Mexico.

Utah's landscapes include mountains and hot, dry deserts. The Rocky Mountains cut through the state. Elk, moose, and bears roam the mountains. Wildflowers grow there too.

The Colorado Plateau is in southern Utah. This is a high area of land with many canyons. The Basin and Range region of western Utah is flat. This region is home to the Great Salt Lake.

Utah's Climate

Utah experiences all four seasons. But the climate also varies across the state.

The Great Salt Lake

Thousands of years ago, Lake Bonneville covered 20,000 square miles (51,800 sq km) of land. Over time, the lake **evaporated**. The Great Salt Lake is the only part of the original lake that remains. White salt covers the ground where Lake Bonneville used to be. This area is called the Bonneville Salt Flats.

Utah's Dead Horse Point State Park is part of the Colorado Plateau. The Colorado River runs through the plateau and creates wide canyons.

Utahns claim to have the Greatest Snow on Earth. The state's climate creates snow that is ideal for winter sports such as skiing.

Winters are usually snowy in the state's mountainous regions. During a typical winter, about 5 feet (1.5 m) of snow falls in Utah's mountains.

Other parts of Utah are among the driest places in the United States. Southern Utah has

The Great Salt Lake is the eighth largest saltwater lake in the world.

a desertlike climate. Summers are very hot. Temperatures are milder in the spring and autumn. Lots of sunshine draws people outside.

Further Evidence

Visit the website below. Does it give any new evidence to support Chapter One?

Utah

abdocorelibrary.com/discovering-utah

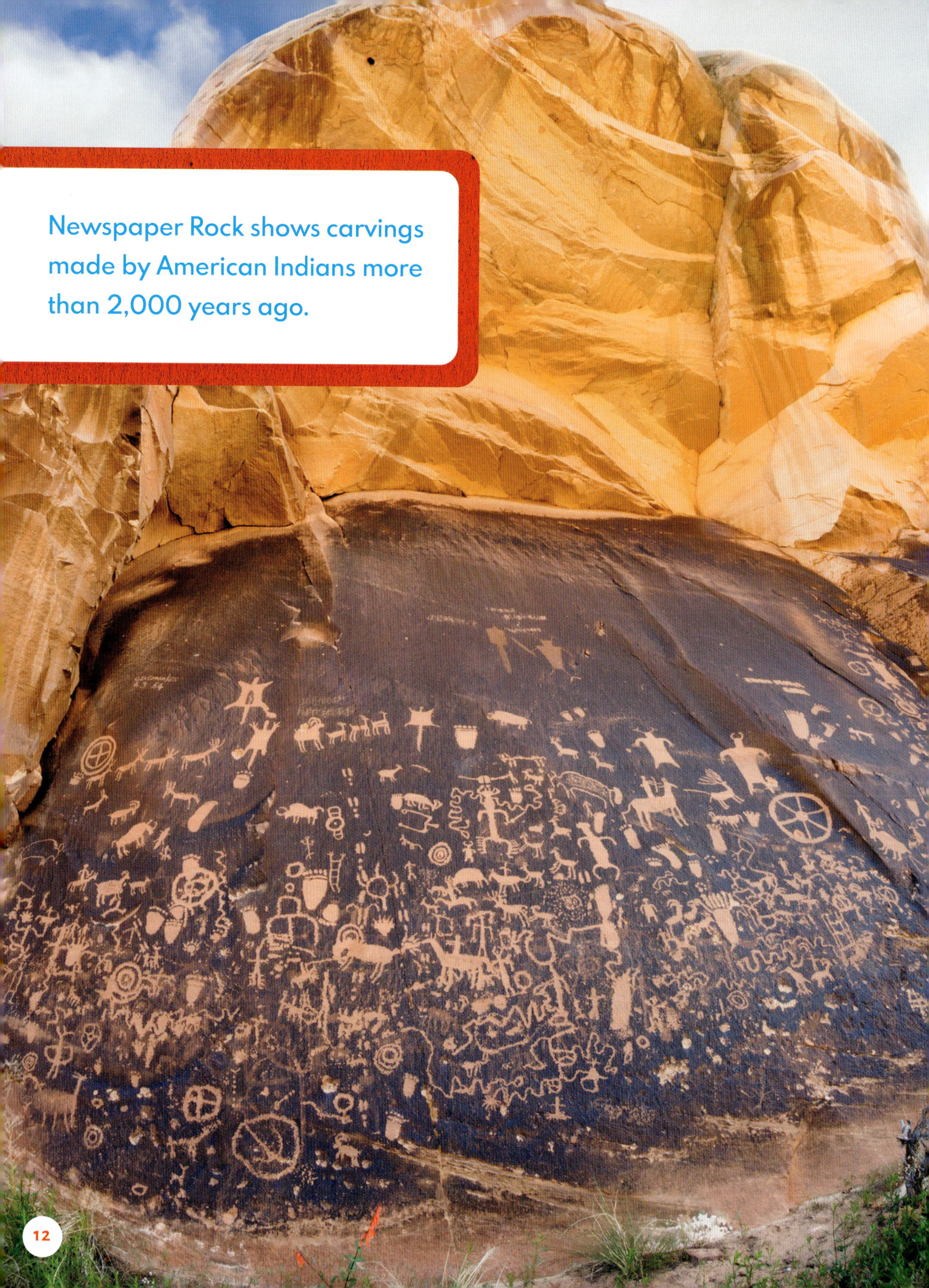

Newspaper Rock shows carvings made by American Indians more than 2,000 years ago.

CHAPTER 2

The People of Utah

Humans have lived in Utah for more than 11,000 years. The first American Indian people in Utah hunted and gathered food. About 2,500 years ago, some people began to farm. In southern Utah, the Ancestral Pueblo peoples lived among rock cliffs.

Utah's state flag shows a beehive. Utah is known as the Beehive State. This symbol comes from the Church of Jesus Christ of Latter-day Saints. It represents working together.

Other American Indian peoples in Utah include the Shoshone, Paiute, and Goshute. Today, the US government recognizes eight American Indian nations in Utah.

Immigration

In the mid-1800s, members of the Church of Jesus Christ of Latter-day Saints were looking for a place to practice their religion. They chose the Great Salt Lake valley. Salt Lake City still has a large population of Latter-day Saints.

Today, nearly 77 percent of Utahns are white. About 15 percent are Hispanic or Latino, and 1.6 percent are Black. Almost 3 percent are Asian, and 1.5 percent are American Indian. About 3.38 million people live in Utah.

Culture

Utah's past still plays an important part in the state's culture. Many Latter-day Saints don't drink coffee or tea for religious reasons.

But soda shops are popular in Utah. Visitors mix flavored syrups with their favorite drinks.

Sports are another part of Utah's culture. For a long time, the state's only professional sports team was the Utah Jazz basketball team. Utah now has men's and women's soccer teams.

Sundance Film Festival

Park City, Utah, hosts the Sundance Film Festival. Sundance is the largest independent film festival in the United States. Films shown there are made by independent studios rather than big Hollywood filmmakers. The festival is important for these small studios. It helps audiences learn about smaller films. Many famous films have **premiered** at Sundance.

The Utah Jazz play at Delta Center in Salt Lake City.

Copper is a major product mined in Utah.

Rugby is another growing sport. Fans cheer on Utah's Major League Rugby team, the Utah Warriors.

Winter sports are also popular in Utah. Millions of people ski and snowboard down Utah's slopes each year. Some famous winter sports athletes have come from Utah. Noelle Pikus-Pace was born in Provo. She became an Olympic **skeleton** racer.

Industry

During the 1860s, small amounts of gold and silver were discovered in the Wasatch Mountains. Soon Utah's mines were world famous. Mining is still an important part of Utah's economy.

Some Utahns work as tour guides. They lead people in activities such as kayaking.

Many Utahns work in finance and **manufacturing**. Since Utah is a popular vacation spot, many Utahns have jobs in tourism. They work at ski resorts, hotels, or restaurants.

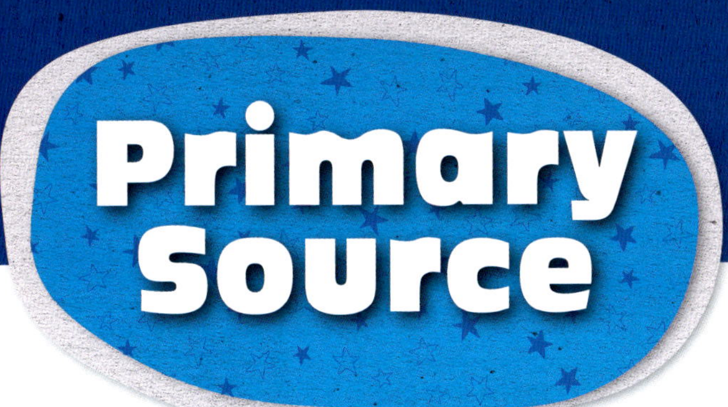

Swig is a popular soda shop chain in Utah. Nicole Tanner founded the store. She spoke about how the store became popular:

> When we first started in 2010, we called one of our drinks a Dirty Dr. Pepper—which is just coconut syrup in a Dr. Pepper. People thought it was the coolest thing.

Source: Nicole Tanner. "How Nicole Tanner Founded Swig." *Utah Business*, 4 Aug. 2022, utahbusiness.org. Accessed 22 Nov. 2023.

Comparing Texts

Think about the quote. Does it support the information in this chapter? Or does it give a different perspective? Explain how in a few sentences.

The Utah State Capitol building stands in Salt Lake City. Its dome is covered in copper mined in Utah.

CHAPTER 3

Places in Utah

There are many interesting places to visit in Utah. Salt Lake City is Utah's capital. The city lies in a valley surrounded by mountains. Visitors can see the Salt Lake Temple in Salt Lake City. This temple is important to many Latter-day Saints.

Delicate Arch is one of more than 2,000 rock arches in Arches National Park.

South of Salt Lake City lies Provo. Provo borders Utah Lake. The city is home to Brigham Young University. The university has several museums. One is the Museum of Peoples and Cultures. Exhibits teach visitors about the peoples who have lived in Utah.

Parks and Landmarks

Utah has five national parks. All five are in southern Utah. Each has something special.

Arches National Park is known for its red stone arches. These can be up to 112 feet (34 m) tall. At Bryce Canyon National Park, sandstone columns stick out of the ground. Rivers have carved out the land in Canyonlands National Park. At Capitol Reef National Park, visitors can see a wrinkle in the Earth's **crust**. Zion National Park is known for its forests and waterfalls.

The Four Corners

The southeastern tip of Utah touches the tips of New Mexico, Colorado, and Arizona. This location is called the Four Corners Monument. Four Corners is the only place in the country where four states come together. If visitors stand in just the right place, they can be in multiple states at once.

In 1965, Bobby Summers broke a land speed record at the Bonneville Salt Flats. He drove more than 400 miles per hour (640 km/h).

Utah has many other natural landmarks. In northern Utah, people can visit Dinosaur National Monument. This is a **quarry** filled with dinosaur **fossils**.

West of Salt Lake City are the Bonneville Salt Flats. Some people come to the Salt Flats to race cars and motorcycles. Drivers have set many speed records there.

Utah has a diverse history. People can learn about those who have called the state home. They can also see the state's natural beauty or ski down its famous mountains. There is something for everyone in Utah.

Explore Online

Dinosaur National Monument draws hundreds of thousands of visitors each year. Visit the website below. What new information have you learned about the dinosaurs of Utah?

Dinosaur National Monument

abdocorelibrary.com/discovering-utah

State Map

Provo

Bryce Canyon National Park

KEY

 Capital
 Park

City or town
 Point of interest

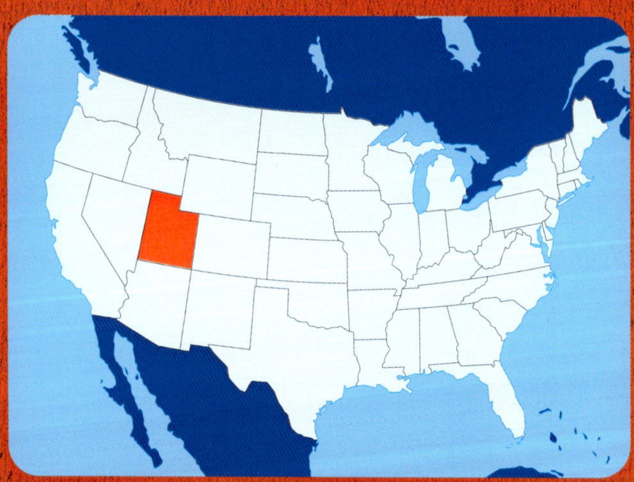

Great Salt Lake

Zion National Park

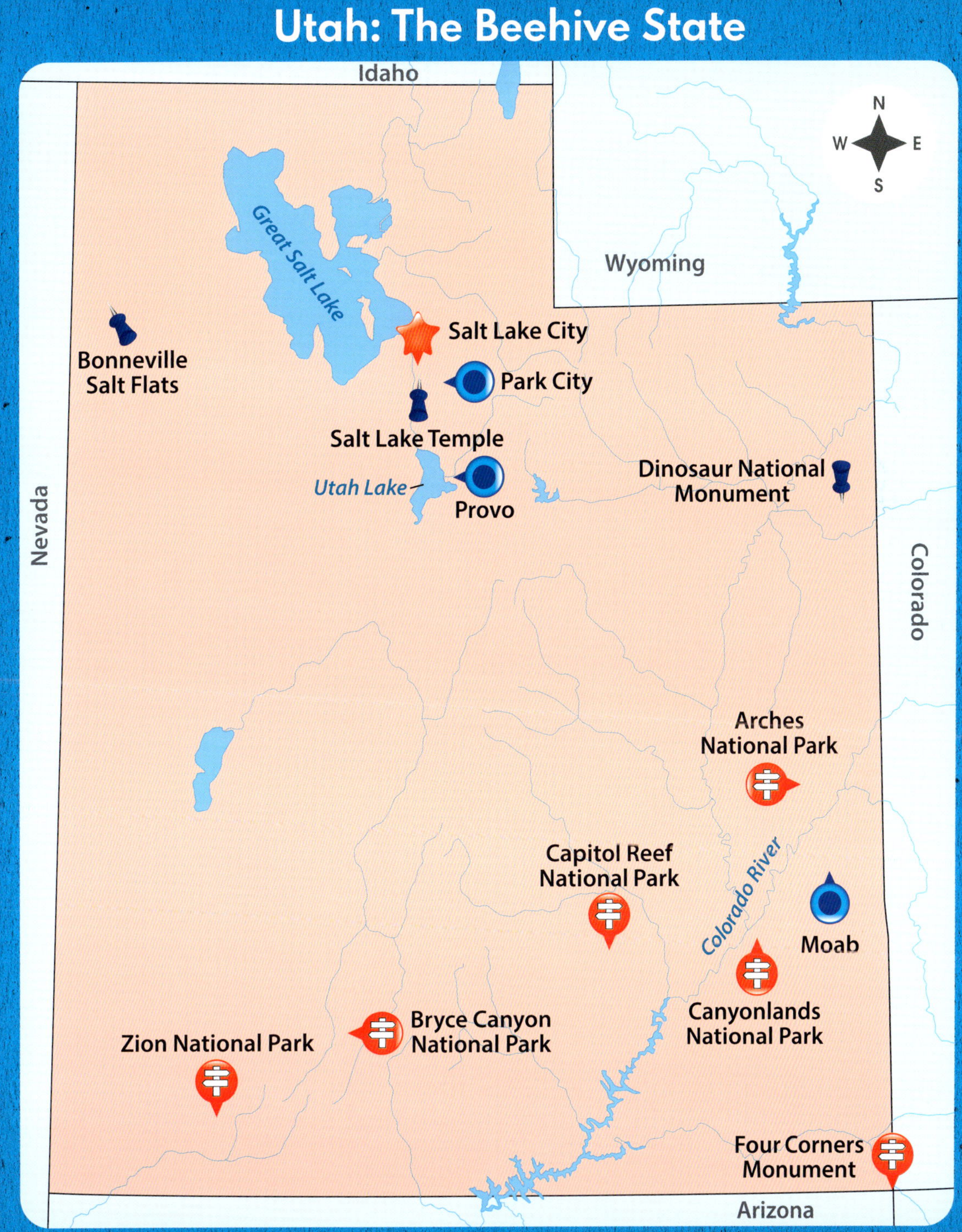
Utah: The Beehive State
Idaho
N
W
E
S
Great Salt Lake
Wyoming
Salt Lake City
Bonneville
Salt Flats
Park City
Salt Lake Temple
Utah Lake
Provo
Dinosaur National
Monument
Nevada
Colorado
Arches
National Park
Capitol Reef
National Park
Colorado River
Moab
Canyonlands
National Park
Bryce Canyon
National Park
Zion National Park
Four Corners
Monument
Arizona

Glossary

crust
the outer shell of a planet

evaporated
turned into gas

fossils
the very old, preserved remains of animals or plants

manufacturing
the process of making goods to sell

premiered
showed for the first time

quarry
a large, deep pit usually made by digging for something

skeleton
a winter sport where athletes race headfirst on sleds down an icy course

Online Resources

To learn more about Utah, visit our free resource websites below.

Visit **abdocorelibrary.com** or scan this QR code for free Common Core resources for teachers and students, including vetted activities, multimedia, and booklinks, for deeper subject comprehension.

Visit **abdobooklinks.com** or scan this QR code for free additional online weblinks for further learning. These links are routinely monitored and updated to provide the most current information available.

Learn More

Avise, Jonathan. *Utah Jazz.* Abdo, 2023.

Morey, Allan. *Snowboarding.* Abdo, 2021.

Payne, Stefanie. *The National Parks.* DK, 2020.

Index

About the Author

Blythe Lawrence is a journalist from Seattle, Washington. She often writes about Olympic sports and history.